U.S. Department of Justice
Office of Justice Programs
Office of Juvenile Justice and Delinquency Prevention

Shay Bilchik, Administrator

August 1998

JUVENILE JUSTICE BULLETIN

Youth Gangs: An Overview

James C. Howell

The proliferation of youth gangs since 1980 has fueled the public's fear and magnified possible misconceptions about youth gangs. To address the mounting concern about youth gangs, the Office of Juvenile Justice and Delinquency Prevention (OJJDP) has initiated the Youth Gang Series to delve into many of the key issues related to youth gangs. These issues include gang migration, gang growth, female involvement with gangs, homicide, drugs and violence, and the needs of communities and youth who live in the presence of youth gangs. This Bulletin, the first in the series, provides an overview of the problems that youth gangs pose, pinpoints the differences between youth gangs and adult criminal organizations, examines the risk factors that lead to youth gang membership, and presents promising strategies being used to curb youth gang involvement.

Introduction

The United States has seen rapid proliferation of youth gangs[1] since 1980. During this period, the number of cities with gang problems increased from an estimated 286 jurisdictions with more than 2,000 gangs and nearly 100,000 gang members in 1980 (Miller, 1992) to about 4,800 jurisdictions with more than 31,000 gangs and approximately 846,000 gang members in 1996 (Moore and Terrett, in press).[2] An 11-city survey of eighth graders found that 9

percent were currently gang members, and 17 percent said they had belonged to a gang at some point in their lives (Esbensen and Osgood, 1997).

Other studies reported comparable percentages and also showed that gang members were responsible for a large proportion of violent offenses. In the Rochester site of the OJJDP-funded Program of Research on the Causes and Correlates of Delinquency, gang members (30 percent of the sample) self-reported committing

---

[1] This overview relies on definitions of the term "youth gang" offered by the leading gang theorists and researchers. For the purposes of this review, a group must be involved in a pattern of criminal acts to be considered a youth gang. These groups are typically composed only of juveniles, but may include young adults in their membership. Prison gangs, ideological gangs, hate groups, and motorcycle gangs are not included. Likewise, gangs whose membership is restricted to adults and that do not have the characteristics of youth gangs are excluded (see Curry and Decker, 1998). **Unless otherwise noted, the term "gangs" refers to youth gangs.**

[2] Sheriff's departments were asked to report data only on unincorporated areas in an effort to reduce redundancies. Respondents were allowed to use their own definition of a gang, with the guidance that "youth gang" was defined as "a group of youths in the [respondent's] jurisdiction that the [respondent or other] responsible persons in the [respondent's] agency or community are willing to identify or classify as a 'gang'." Motorcycle gangs, hate or ideology groups, prison gangs, and adult gangs were excluded. See Moore (1997) and National Youth Gang Center (1997) for results of the 1995 National Youth Gang Survey.

From the Administrator

Despite recent declines in juvenile crime, our Nation continues to face a youth gang problem. As part of our response to public concern about this problem, OJJDP has initiated the Youth Gang Series to explore key issues related to youth gangs. These issues include gang migration, female involvement with gangs, and the growth of gang activity related to homicide, drugs, and overall delinquency.

Youth Gangs: An Overview, the initial Bulletin in this series, brings together available knowledge on youth gangs by reviewing data and research. The author begins with a look at the history of youth gangs and their demographic characteristics. He then assesses the scope of the youth gang problem, including gang problems in juvenile detention and correctional facilities. A review of gang studies provides a clearer understanding of several issues. An extensive list of references is also included for further review.

The Bulletin makes a clear statement that a successful gang intervention and suppression strategy must build on services already in place in our communities to develop a comprehensive approach that will enhance the capacity of the juvenile justice system. The information provided here and in subsequent titles of this series will serve as a good starting point toward that end.

Shay Bilchik
Administrator

68 percent of all violent offenses (Thornberry, 1998). In the Denver site, adolescent gang members (14 percent of the sample) self-reported committing 89 percent of all serious violent offenses (Huizinga, 1997). In another study, supported by OJJDP and several other agencies and organizations, adolescent gang members in Seattle (15 percent of the sample) self-reported involvement in 85 percent of robberies committed by the entire sample (Battin et al., 1998).

This Bulletin reviews data and research to consolidate available knowledge on youth gangs that are involved in criminal activity. Following a historical perspective, demographic information is presented. The scope of the problem is assessed, including gang problems in juvenile detention and correctional facilities. Several issues are then addressed by reviewing gang studies to provide a clearer understanding of youth gang problems. An extensive list of references is provided for further review.

History of Youth Gangs

Youth gangs may have first appeared in Europe (Klein, 1996) or Mexico (Redfield, 1941; Rubel, 1965). No one is sure when or why they emerged in the United States. The earliest record of their appearance in the United States may have been as early as 1783, as the American Revolution ended (Sante, 1991; Sheldon, 1898). They may have emerged spontaneously from adolescent play groups or as a collective response to urban conditions in this country (Thrasher, 1927). Some suggest they first emerged following the Mexican migration to the Southwest after the Mexican Revolution in 1813 (Redfield, 1941; Rubel, 1965). They may have grown out of difficulties Mexican youth encountered with social and cultural adjustment to the American way of life under extremely poor conditions in the Southwest (Moore, 1978; Vigil, 1988). Gangs appear to have spread in New England in the early 1800's as the Industrial Revolution gained momentum in the first large cities in the United States: New York, Boston, and Philadelphia (Finestone, 1976; Sante, 1991; Spergel, 1995).

Gangs began to flourish in Chicago and other large cities during the industrial era, when immigration and population shifts reached peak levels (Finestone, 1976). Early in American history, gangs seem to have been most visible and most violent during periods of rapid population shifts. Their evolution has been characterized by an ebb and flow pattern that "at any given time more closely resembles that of, say, influenza rather than blindness," as Miller (1992:51) has observed. The United States has seen four distinct periods of gang growth and peak activity: the late 1800's, the 1920's, the 1960's, and the 1990's (Curry and Decker, 1998). Gang proliferation, in other words, is not a constant.

In the modern era, youth gangs have been influenced by several trends. In the 1970's and 1980's, because of increased mobility and access to more lethal weapons, many gangs became more dangerous (Klein, 1995; Klein and Maxson, 1989; Miller, 1974, 1992; Spergel, 1995). Gang fights previously involving fists or brass knuckles increasingly involved guns. The growing availability of automobiles, coupled with the use of more lethal weapons, fueled the growth of drive-by shootings, a tactic that previously took the form of on-foot hit-and-run forays (Miller, 1966). Gangs of the 1980's and 1990's seem to have both more younger and more older members than before (Miller, 1992; Spergel, 1995), more members with prison records or ties to prison inmates (Hagedorn, 1988; Miller, 1992; Moore, 1990; Vigil, 1988), and more weapons of greater lethality (Block and Block, 1993; Miller, 1992; National Drug Intelligence Center, 1995). They are less concerned with territorial affiliations (Fagan, 1990; Klein, 1995), use alcohol and drugs more extensively (Decker and Van Winkle, 1996; Fagan, 1990; Thornberry, 1998), and are more involved in drug trafficking (Battin et al., 1998; Fagan, 1990; Miller, 1992; Taylor, 1989; Thornberry, 1998).

Some youth gangs appear to have been transformed into entrepreneurial organizations by the crack cocaine epidemic that began in the mid-1980's (Sanchez-Jankowski, 1991; Skolnick et al., 1988; Taylor, 1989). However, the extent to which they have become drug-trafficking organizations is unclear (Howell and Decker, in press). Some youth groups, many of which are not considered bona fide gangs, are not seriously involved in illegal activities and provide mainly social opportunities for their membership (Fagan, 1989; Vigil, 1988). Some gangs seldom use drugs and alcohol, and some have close community ties (Fagan, 1989; Sanchez-Jankowski, 1991; Vigil, 1988).

Demographic Characteristics

The average age of youth gang members is about 17 to 18 years (Curry and Decker, 1998), but tends to be older in cities in which gangs have been in existence longer, like Chicago and Los Angeles (Bobrowski, 1988; California Attorney General's Gang Unit, 1996; Klein, 1995; Spergel, 1995). The typical age range is 12 to 24. Although younger members are becoming more common, it is the older membership that has increased the most (Hagedorn, 1988; Moore, 1990; Spergel, 1995). Male gang members outnumber females by a wide margin (Miller, 1992; Moore, 1978), and this span is greater in late adolescence than in early adolescence (Bjerregaard and Smith, 1993; Esbensen and Huizinga, 1993; Moore and Hagedorn, 1996). Gangs vary in size by type of gang. Traditional (large, enduring, territorial) gangs average about 180 members, whereas specialty (e.g., drug trafficking) gangs average only about 25 members (Klein and Maxson, 1996). In large cities, some gangs number in the thousands and even tens of thousands (Block and Block, 1993; Spergel, 1995).

In the early 19th century, youth gangs in the United States were primarily Irish, Jewish, and Italian (Haskins, 1974; Sante, 1991). According to a recent national law enforcement survey, the ethnicity of gang members is 48 percent African-American, 43 percent Hispanic,[3] 5 percent white, and 4 percent Asian (Curry, 1996). However, student surveys show a much larger representation of white adolescents among gang members. In a survey of nearly 6,000 eighth graders in 11 sites (Esbensen and Osgood, 1997), 31 percent of the students who said they were gang members were African-American, 25 percent were Hispanic, 25 percent were white, 5 percent were Asian, and 15 percent were of other racial and ethnic groups.[4] Bursik and Grasmick (1993) point out that, despite the disproportionate representation of minority group members in studies as compared with white youth, "blacks and Hispanics have no special predisposition to gang membership. Rather, they simply are overrepresented in those areas most likely to lead to gang activity."

Miller (1974:220) notes that "observers of any given period tend to relate the characteristics of gangs to those of the particular ethnic groups prominent in the urban lower class during that period . . . , roughly, the more prevalent the lower-class

---

[3] Hispanic (Spanish-speaking) ethnic groups include Mexicans, Mexican-Americans, Latinos, and Puerto Ricans.

[4] Percentages total to 101 due to rounding.

populations, the more gangs." Spergel (1995:60) agrees, but with an important caveat: "Contemporary youth gangs are located primarily in lower-class, slum, ghetto, barrio, or working-class changing communities, but it is not clear that either class, poverty, culture, race or ethnicity, or social change per se primarily accounts [sic] for gang problems." Spergel's observation appears to be correct, because gangs have recently become much more prevalent in rural counties, small cities, and towns (Moore and Terrett, in press), for reasons that are not well understood.

Gang Specialization

Certain offenses are related to different racial/ethnic youth gangs. African-American gangs are relatively more involved in drug offenses; Hispanic gangs, in "turf-related" violence; Asian and white gangs, in property crimes (Block et al., 1996; Spergel, 1990). Numerous ethnographic studies have provided excellent descriptions of Hispanic gangs in Los Angeles. They tend to be structured around age-based cohorts, based in a specific territory (barrio), and characterized by fighting (Moore, Vigil, and Garcia, 1983). The gang provides family-like relationships for adolescents who feel isolated, drifting between their native and adopted cultures and feeling alienated from both (Vigil, 1990a, 1990b; Vigil and Long, 1990). Hispanic gangs have strong links to the neighborhood, or barrio, which tie them to the larger culture (Moore, 1978); much of their violence is related to defense of neighborhood turf. In contrast, African-American gangs in large cities tend to replace traditional social networks that linked youth with legitimate work opportunities (Anderson, 1990). Thus, these gangs tend to be involved in entrepreneurial activities more than other ethnic/racial gangs and may evolve from "scavenger" groups to turf gangs and drug-trafficking gangs (Taylor, 1989).

Use of violence to protect the neighborhood, or gang turf, from rival gangs is also a predominant goal in Chicago (Block and Block, 1993), San Diego (Pennell et al., 1994), and St. Louis (Decker and Van Winkle, 1996). Violence is rarely planned and generally occurs spontaneously among gangs (Decker and Van Winkle, 1996; Sanchez-Jankowski, 1991; Pennell et al., 1994) in response to a wide variety of situations (Horowitz and Schwartz, 1974; Sanders, 1994).

Numerous ways of classifying gangs other than by ethnicity have been devised (Spergel, 1995), although the gangs' com-

plexity, variations, and changing structure practically defy static categories. One way of viewing gangs is along a continuum of degree of organization (Gordon, 1994), from youth groups who hang out together in shopping malls and other places; to criminal groups, small clusters of friends who band together to commit crimes such as fencing operations; to street gangs composed of groups of adolescents and young adults who form a semistructured operation and engage in delinquent and criminal behavior; to adult criminal organizations that engage in criminal activity primarily for economic reasons. The latter, also called criminal gangs, are not considered youth gangs. Distinguishing among these various forms of gangs is often not easy; in some areas, groups may evolve from less formal to more formal organizations along this continuum.

Female Gang Delinquency

Data on the number of female youth gang members have not yet been gathered nationwide; however, several estimates are available. Miller (1992) estimated that approximately 10 percent of gang members were females. Among law enforcement agencies that reported male and female membership data in a 1992 survey, gang membership was estimated to be nearly 6 percent female (Curry, 1995b). In their 11-city survey of eighth graders, Esbensen and Osgood (1997) report that 38 percent of the students who said they were gang members were females. Recent studies of large adolescent samples in urban areas, funded through OJJDP's Program of Research on the Causes and Correlates of Delinquency, report that female membership is higher in early adolescence (Bjerregaard and Smith, 1993; Esbensen and Huizinga, 1993). Among all adolescents, female involvement may be increasing proportionally with male gang involvement (Klein, 1995). Surveys have been incapable of measuring these changes nationwide because data and information systems at the local level are inadequate. Nevertheless, these and other studies of urban samples (Fagan, 1990; Winfree et al., 1992) suggest growing involvement of females in gangs concomitant with gang proliferation.

Are independent female gangs increasing? The initial survey of cities with gang problems indicates that by far the most common female gangs are auxiliary gangs affiliated with male gangs (Miller, 1975). Subsequent surveys suggest an increase in independent female gangs (Curry, Ball,

and Decker, 1996; Curry, 1995a, 1995b; National Drug Intelligence Center, 1995). However, Moore (1991:41) suggests that "the general notion that gang girls have moved away from . . . 'traditional [auxiliary] roles' must be taken with a grain of salt." Based on her review of gang research, Chesney-Lind (1993) contends that there is little evidence to support the notion of a new breed of violent female gangsters breaking into this historically male-dominated phenomenon.

Are female gang members becoming involved in more serious and violent offending? This question cannot be answered definitively because national trend data are not available. Chicago data on gang-related offenses during the 30-year period from 1965 to 1994 show that females represented only 5 percent of victims and 1 percent of offenders (Block et al., 1996). Female gang violence was more likely to involve simple battery or assault rather than homicide, and female nonviolent crimes consisted mainly of liquor law violations.

In the OJJDP-funded Causes and Correlates study site of Denver, Esbensen and Huizinga (1993) found that delinquent behavior was much more prevalent among female gang members than nongang females. However, incidence rates were not significantly higher. In Rochester, another Causes and Correlates study site, Bjerregaard and Smith (1993) also found that female gang members were significantly more likely to engage in serious delinquency than nongang females. However, in contrast to Denver, the incidence rates in Rochester in every offense category were significantly higher among female gang members than among nongang females. Fagan (1990) also found high levels of involvement in serious delinquency among female gang members in Chicago, Los Angeles, and San Diego. Prevalence rates in all behavior categories, including violent offenses, were higher among female gang members than among nongang males.

Scope of the Problem

Assessing the scope of the youth gang problem in the United States is difficult. No consensus exists on what constitutes a youth gang. Many jurisdictions deny the existence of gangs. Others incorrectly, many experts believe, characterize less serious forms of adolescent law-violating groups as gangs (Miller, 1992). Some call gangs by other names, such as "crews" or "posses," although some of these are not bona fide gangs; rather, they are specialized groups engaged in predatory crimes or drug trafficking (Miller, 1992). It appears that communities are likely to label troublesome adolescent groups as gangs if the public perceives them to be a problem (Miller, 1992). Although youth gang definitions vary, most include the following elements: a self-formed group, united by mutual interests, that controls a particular territory, facility, or enterprise; uses symbols in communications; and is collectively involved in crime (Curry and Decker, 1998; Miller, 1992).

Youth Gang Proliferation

Few systematic data are collected routinely on youth gangs at the city or county level, with the exception of a few gang information systems. In the past, intermittent surveys were relied on for assessing the national scope of the gang problem (Curry et al., 1992; Curry, Ball, and Decker, 1996; Klein, 1995; Knox et al., 1996; Miller, 1975, 1992; Needle and Stapleton, 1983). In 1996, the National Youth Gang Center surveyed more than 3,000 law enforcement agencies, 87 percent of which responded, to obtain a more complete count of jurisdictions with gang problems (Moore and Terrett, in press).

Almost three-fourths of cities surveyed with populations of 25,000 or more reported youth gangs in 1996 (Moore and Terrett, in press). Respondents in large cities reported the highest level of gang activity (74 percent), followed by suburban counties (57 percent), small cities (34 percent), and rural counties (25 percent). Most respondents reported that their gang problem began quite recently, with 1994 the most frequently cited year. The *average* year of onset varied with the type of locality: 1989 for large cities, 1990 for suburban counties, 1992 for small cities, and 1993 for rural counties. Thus, the youth gang problem in this country is substantial and affects communities of all sizes.

Youth gangs are especially widespread in certain cities with chronic gang problems such as Chicago (Block et al., 1996) and Los Angeles (Klein, 1995). Chicago is said to have about 132 gangs (Block et al., 1996), with an estimated membership of 30,000 to 50,000 hardcore gang members (Chicago Crime Commission, 1995). Members of Chicago's four largest and most criminally active gangs, the Black Gangster Disciples Nation, the Latin Disciples, the Latin Kings, and the Vice Lords, number about 19,000 and account for two-thirds of all gang-motivated crimes and for more than half of the city's gang-motivated homicides (Block and Block, 1993). Police in Los Angeles estimate that the city has more than 58,000 gang members (National Youth Gang Center, 1997), making it the U.S. city with the most gang members.

Gang Problems in Juvenile Detention and Correctional Facilities

Three surveys have assessed youth gang problems in juvenile detention and correctional facilities. The OJJDP-funded Conditions of Confinement: Juvenile Detention and Corrections Facilities study (Parent et al., 1994) included a survey of all detention and correctional facility administrators. Administrators in detention centers and training schools were asked to estimate the proportion of confined juveniles who had problems in particular areas, including gang involvement. In both the detention center and training school populations, facility administrators estimated that about 40 percent of the confined youth were involved in gangs (Leiter, 1993, cited in Snyder and Sickmund, 1995).

A 1990 Juvenile Correctional Institutions Survey (Knox, 1991) found that 160 respondents, more than three-fourths (78 percent) of responding institutions, reported a gang problem for some period of time. Fifty-two percent of the responding institutions reported that more than 10 percent of confined youth were involved in gangs. More than one-third (40 percent) reported gang involvement of female inmates. The survey inquired about problems gangs presented in the institutions. Assaults on correctional officers were reported by 14 percent of respondents; among these, 28 percent reported more than one incident. Of the 150 reported assaults on correctional officers, 11 resulted in hospitalization. Approximately one-third of all responding institutions reported one or more incidents in which violence involving gang members resulted in serious injury.

In a sample of inner-city high schools and juvenile correctional facilities in 4 States, Sheley and Wright (1993, 1995) surveyed more than 800 male serious offenders in 6 juvenile correctional facilities located near urban areas experiencing youth gang problems. Two-thirds (68 percent) of the inmates self-reported affiliation with a gang or a "quasi-gang." Gang members were much more likely than nongang members to have possessed guns: 81 percent of gang and quasi-gang members owned a revolver, and about three-fourths owned an automatic or semiautomatic handgun. Eighty-four percent of the inmates said they carried a gun at least "now and then" in the year or two before being incarcerated, and 55 percent said "all" or "most of the time."

Gangs clearly present significant problems in juvenile detention and correctional facilities. There is evidence that, in addition to contributing to institutional violence, gangs form in these facilities and recruit members there (Moore, Vigil, and Garcia, 1983). The formation of gangs probably is related to inmates' need for protection from other inmates. The Chicago Vice Lords originated in the Illinois State Training School for Boys when several residents decided to form a new gang by pooling their affiliations with other gangs, hoping to form the toughest gang in Chicago (Dawley, 1992; Keiser, 1969). Confinement in a juvenile correctional facility is one of the strongest predictors of adult prison gang membership (Ralph et al., 1996).

Programs are needed to break the cycle of street-level youth gang involvement, further involvement in juvenile detention and correctional facilities and prisons, and continued gang involvement in the communities to which former inmates return.

Community and Economy

A major source of variation in youth gang violence is found in relationships between the gang and the community. J.F. Short, Jr., contends that the concept of gangs used in gang research is too narrow, in that it does not take into account the relevance of gangs and gang membership in other social settings (personal communication to the author, April 24, 1996). First, the gang's relevance goes beyond its relationship to individual gang members. For example, gangs serve as carriers of community traditions and culture (Miller, 1958; Moore, 1978). Second, a youth's identification with a gang affects how others react to him or her. To illustrate, Esbensen and Huizinga (1993) found that negative labeling of gang members is linked to elevated offenses.

Much remains to be learned about the relationship between gangs and their neighborhoods or communities. Sanchez-Jankowski (1991) identified four factors that motivate gangs to make concerted efforts to establish ties with the community. First, the gang needs a "safe haven." Second, it needs a recruitment pool from which to draw its membership. Third, the community provides the gang with important information (e.g., on gangs in other parts of the city). Fourth, the gang needs the community ties for psychological reasons: "A bonding occurs between the gang and the community that builds a social adhesive that often takes a significant amount of time to completely dissolve" (Sanchez-Jankowski, 1991:201). These are important features of youth gangs. Sanchez-Jankowski (1991) has argued that community ambivalence toward gangs exists because many of the gang members are children of residents, the gangs often provide protection for residents, residents identify with gangs because of their own or relatives' prior involvement, and the gangs in some instances have become community institutions; personal interests (fear of too much policing, fear of too much gang activity) also figure in community perceptions of gangs.

Another reason for ambivalence toward, or acceptance of, gangs could be the changing economy. Recent gang theory has focused on the effects of the changing urban economy on gang-neighborhood dynamics (Bursik and Grasmick, 1993). The transition during the 1970's from a manufacturing to a service-based economy in the United States drastically changed economic conditions, reducing the demand for low-skilled workers in an increasingly

service-oriented, high-tech society, restricting their access to the labor market, and blocking their upward mobility, creating what Glasgow (1980) first called the underclass (see also Wilson, 1987, 1996). Fagan (1996) describes the underclass' plight as being permanently excluded from participating in mainstream labor market occupations. As a result, members of the underclass must rely on other economic alternatives: low-paying temporary jobs, part-time jobs in the secondary labor market, some form of welfare or dependence on friends and relatives, or involvement in drug trafficking and other profitable street crimes (Moore, 1988). Several gang researchers (Bursik and Grasmick, 1993; Decker, 1996; Hagedorn, 1988; Moore, 1978, 1985; Sullivan 1989; Vigil, 1988) have argued that crime, delinquency, gangs, and youth violence have increased in the 1980's and 1990's as a result of these postindustrial society conditions.

Why Do Youth Join Gangs?

Decker and Van Winkle (1996) view joining youth gangs as consisting of both pulls and pushes. Pulls pertain to the attractiveness of the gang. Gang membership can enhance prestige or status among friends (Baccaglini, 1993), especially girls (for boys) (Decker and Van Winkle, 1996), and provide opportunities to be with them (Slayton, Stephens, and MacKenna, 1993). Gangs provide other attractive opportunities such as the chance for excitement (Pennell et al., 1994) by selling drugs and making money (Decker and Van Winkle, 1996). Thus, many youth see themselves as making a rational

choice in deciding to join a gang: They see personal advantages to gang membership (Sanchez-Jankowski, 1991).

Social, economic, and cultural forces push many adolescents in the direction of gangs. Protection from other gangs and perceived general well-being are key factors (Baccaglini, 1993; Decker and Van Winkle, 1996). As noted above, some researchers contend that the "underclass" (Wilson, 1987) status of minority youth serves to push them into gangs (Hagedorn, 1988; Moore, 1978; Taylor, 1989; Vigil, 1988). Feeling marginal, adolescents join gangs for social relationships that give them a sense of identity (Vigil and Long, 1990). For some youth, gangs provide a way of solving social adjustment problems, particularly the trials and tribulations of adolescence (Short and Strodtbeck, 1965). In some communities, youth are intensively recruited or coerced into gangs (Johnstone, 1983). They seemingly have no choice. A few are virtually born into gangs as a result of neighborhood traditions and their parents' earlier (and perhaps continuing) gang participation or involvement in criminal activity (Moore, 1978).

Risk Factors for Gang Membership

Table 1 summarizes risk factors for youth gang membership that have been identified in studies using many types of research methods, including cross-sectional, longitudinal, and ethnographic (observational) studies. Examination of this table suggests that the present state of knowledge of risk factors for gang membership is not refined. Because so many risk factors have been identified,

Table 1: Risk Factors for Youth Gang Membership

Domain	Risk Factors	Sources
Community	Social disorganization, including poverty and residential mobility	Curry and Spergel, 1988
	Organized lowerclass communities	Miller, 1958; Moore, 1991
	Underclass communities	Bursik and Grasmick, 1993; Hagedorn, 1988; Moore, 1978, 1985, 1988, 1991; Moore, Vigil, and Garcia, 1983; Sullivan, 1989
	Presence of gangs in the neighborhood	Curry and Spergel, 1992
	Availability of drugs in the neighborhood	Curry and Spergel, 1992; Hagedorn, 1988, 1994a, 1994b; Hill et al., in press; Kosterman et al., 1996; Moore, 1978, 1991; Sanchez-Jankowski, 1991; Taylor, 1989
	Availability of firearms	Lizotte et al., 1994; Miller, 1992; Newton and Zimring, 1969
	Barriers to and lack of social and economic opportunities	Cloward and Ohlin, 1960; Cohen, 1960; Fagan, 1990; Hagedorn, 1988, 1994b; Klein, 1995; Moore, 1990; Short and Strodtbeck, 1965; Vigil, 1988
	Lack of social capital	Short, 1996; Sullivan, 1989; Vigil, 1988
	Cultural norms supporting gang behavior	Miller, 1958; Short and Strodtbeck, 1965
	Feeling unsafe in neighborhood; high crime	Kosterman et al., 1996; Vigil, 1988
	Conflict with social control institutions	Vigil, 1988
Family	Family disorganization, including broken homes and parental drug/alcohol abuse	Bjerregaard and Smith, 1993; Esbensen, Huizinga, and Weiher, 1993; Hill et al., in press; Vigil, 1988
	Troubled families, including incest, family violence, and drug addiction	Moore, 1978, 1991; Vigil, 1988
	Family members in a gang	Curry and Spergel, 1992; Moore, 1991; Moore, Vigil, and Garcia, 1983
	Lack of adult male role models	Miller, 1958; Vigil, 1988
	Lack of parental role models	Wang, 1995
	Low socioeconomic status	Almost all studies
	Extreme economic deprivation, family management problems, parents with violent attitudes, sibling antisocial behavior	Hill et al., in press; Kosterman et al., 1996
School	Academic failure	Bjerregaard and Smith, 1993; Curry and Spergel, 1992; Kosterman et al., 1996
	Low educational aspirations, especially among females	Bjerregaard and Smith, 1993; Hill et al., in press; Kosterman et al., 1996
	Negative labeling by teachers	Esbensen and Huizinga, 1993; Esbensen, Huizinga, and Weiher, 1993
	Trouble at school	Kosterman et al., 1996
	Few teacher role models	Wang, 1995
	Educational frustration	Curry and Spergel, 1992
	Low commitment to school, low school attachment, high levels of antisocial behavior in school, low achievement test scores, and identification as being learning disabled	Hill et al., in press

Domain	Risk Factors	Sources
Peer Group	High commitment to delinquent peers	Bjerregaard and Smith, 1993; Esbensen and Huizinga, 1993; Vigil and Yun, 1990
	Low commitment to positive peers	Esbensen, Huizinga, and Weiher, 1993
	Street socialization	Vigil, 1988
	Gang members in class	Curry and Spergel, 1992
	Friends who use drugs or who are gang members	Curry and Spergel, 1992
	Friends who are drug distributors	Curry and Spergel, 1992
	Interaction with delinquent peers	Hill et al., in press; Kosterman et al., 1996
Individual	Prior delinquency	Bjerregaard and Smith, 1993; Curry and Spergel, 1992; Esbensen and Huizinga, 1993; Kosterman et al., 1996
	Deviant attitudes	Esbensen, Huizinga, and Weiher, 1993; Fagan, 1990; Hill et al., in press; Kosterman et al., 1996
	Street smartness; toughness	Miller, 1958
	Defiant and individualistic character	Miller, 1958; Sanchez-Jankowski, 1991
	Fatalistic view of the world	Miller, 1958
	Aggression	Campbell, 1984a, 1984b; Cohen, 1960; Horowitz, 1983; Miller, Geertz, and Cutter, 1962; Sanchez-Jankowski, 1991
	Proclivity for excitement and trouble	Miller, 1958; Pennell et al., 1994
	Locura (acting in a daring, courageous, and especially crazy fashion in the face of adversity)	Moore, 1991; Vigil, 1988
	Higher levels of normlessness in the context of family, peer group, and school	Esbensen, Huizinga, and Weiher, 1993
	Social disabilities	Short and Strodtbeck, 1965; Vigil, 1988
	Illegal gun ownership	Bjerregaard and Lizotte, 1995; Lizotte et al., 1994; Vigil and Long, 1990
	Early or precocious sexual activity, especially among females	Kosterman et al., 1996; Bjerregaard and Smith, 1993
	Alcohol and drug use	Bjerregaard and Smith, 1993; Curry and Spergel, 1992; Esbensen, Huizinga, and Weiher, 1993; Hill et al., in press; Thornberry et al., 1993; Vigil and Long, 1990
	Drug trafficking	Fagan, 1990; Thornberry et al., 1993
	Desire for group rewards such as status, identity, self-esteem, companionship, and protection	Curry and Spergel, 1992; Fagan, 1990; Horowitz, 1983; Horowitz and Schwartz, 1974; Moore, 1978, 1991; Short and Strodtbeck, 1965
	Problem behaviors, hyperactivity, externalizing behaviors, drinking, lack of refusal skills, and early sexual activity	Hill et al., in press; Kosterman et al., 1996
	Victimization	Fagan, 1990

it is difficult to determine priorities for gang prevention and intervention programs without an indepth assessment of the crime problem that identifies the most prevalent risk factors.

Long-term studies of large samples of urban adolescents in Rochester, NY (Thornberry, 1998), and Seattle (Hill et al., in press) have identified causal risk factors for gang membership. Both studies, the former funded by OJJDP and the latter supported by OJJDP and other agencies and organizations, measure risk factors in the community, family, school, peer group, and individual attribute domains. Because both studies are collecting data on their respective samples over a long period of time, risk factors measured in early adolescence can be used to predict gang membership at points later in adolescence. The identification of early risk factors indicates priorities for prevention and intervention programs.

In the Rochester study, Thornberry (1998) found predictors of gang membership among males in all five of the domains listed above. The most important community risk factor is growing up in neighborhoods in which the level of social integration (attachment) is low. Neither high levels of neighborhood disorganization nor high levels of violence predict gang membership. Among family variables, poverty, absence of biological parents, low parental attachment to the child, and low parental supervision all increase the probability of gang membership. Three school variables are very significant risk factors: low expectations for success in school (both by parents and students), low student commitment to school, and low attachment to teachers. Along with school factors, peers have a very strong impact on gang membership. Associating with delinquent friends and unsupervised "hanging around" with these delinquent friends are a potent combination. Important individual risk factors identified in the Rochester study are low self-esteem, numerous negative life events, depressive symptoms, and easy access to drugs or favorable views toward drug use. Finally, youth who use drugs and are involved in delinquency—particularly violent delinquency—are more likely to become gang members than are youth who are less involved in delinquency and drug use. In sum, "youth who grow up in more disorganized neighborhoods; who come from impoverished, distressed families; who do poorly in school and have low attachment to school

and teachers; who associate with delinquent peers; and engage in various forms of problem behaviors are at increased risk for becoming gang members" (Thornberry, 1998:157).

Seattle researchers discovered somewhat similar risk factors compared with Thornberry's analysis for both male and female gang membership (Hill et al., in press; Kosterman et al., 1996). The most important community factor identified in the Seattle study is growing up in neighborhoods where drugs are readily available. Several family variables are important: family instability, extreme economic deprivation, family management problems, parents with violent attitudes, and sibling antisocial behavior. Numerous school factors have been identified, including low educational aspiration, low commitment to school, low school attachment, high levels of antisocial behavior in school, low achievement test scores, the identity of being learning disabled, and low grades. The most important peer group factor is associating with law-violating peers. Individual risk factors are the early use of alcohol and marijuana, prior delinquency, hyperactivity, externalizing behaviors (hostility, aggression, and rule breaking), poor skills in refusing offers to engage in antisocial behavior, and early sexual activity. Being a male, feeling unsafe in the neighborhood, and residing in a poor family put youth at high risk for gang involvement, regardless of other community, family, school, or peer risk factors (Kosterman et al., 1996). However, the greater the number of risk factors to which youth are exposed, the greater their risk of joining a gang in adolescence. Children who experience 7 or more risk factors at ages 10 to 12 are 13 times more likely to join a gang in adolescence than children who experience only 1 risk factor or none at those early ages (Hill et al., in press).

Youth Gangs and Violence

Youth gang violence from the 1950's to the 1980's has a curious history. Miller (1992:2) contended that the national perspective of gangs during this period was dominated by a New York City media view: "a flowering in the 1950s, death in the 1960s, revival in the early 1970s, and dormancy in the later 1970s." His survey of gang problems in major American cities (Miller, 1975, 1992) proved the latter part of this media theory to be wrong. Miller's study showed that gang violence was

very prevalent in the 1960's and 1970's. He argued that nothing had changed from the 1950's; rather, media and public attention were diverted from gangs to the Vietnam War, the civil rights movement, and ensuing riots.

Miller's (1992) study indicated that gangs had become more dangerous than ever in the 1970's. He attributed this to four major motives: honor, defense of local turf, control [of facilities], and gain [of money and goods]. In the 1970's, "gang crime was more lethal than any time in history; more people were shot, stabbed, and beaten to death in gang-related incidents than during any previous decade . . . and the prevalence and sophistication of firearms used was unprecedented" (Miller, 1992:142).

Except for gangs that specialize in violence, such as small Chicago Latino gangs (Block et al., 1996), violence is a rare occurrence in proportion to all gang activities (Maxson, 1995; Miller, 1966; Strodtbeck and Short, 1964). It should be noted that violent behavior is not the only behavior in which gang members partake. For the most part, gang members "hang out" and are involved in other normal adolescent social activities, but drinking, drug use, and drug trafficking are also common (Battin et al., 1998; Decker and Van Winkle, 1996; Esbensen, Huizinga, and Weiher, 1993). Although a direct comparison cannot be made, it is apparent that the relative proportion of violence in gang behaviors has increased since the 1950's.

The introduction to this Bulletin notes that youth gang members commit a disproportionate share of offenses, including nonviolent ones. In the Seattle study supported by OJJDP, gang members (15 percent of the sample) self-reported committing 58 percent of general delinquent acts in the entire sample, 51 percent of minor assaults, 54 percent of felony thefts, 53 percent of minor thefts, 62 percent of drug-trafficking offenses, and more than 59 percent of property offenses (Battin et al., 1998). In the OJJDP-funded Causes and Correlates study, Denver gang members (14 percent of the sample) self-reported committing 43 percent of drug sales and 55 percent of all street offenses (Esbensen and Huizinga, 1993). In the same study, Rochester gang members (30 percent of the sample) self-reported committing 70 percent of drug sales, 68 percent of all property offenses, and 86 percent of all serious delinquencies (Thornberry, 1998). Curry, Ball, and Decker (1996) estimated that gang members accounted for nearly 600,000 crimes in 1993.

Gang members also commit serious and violent offenses at a rate several times higher than nongang adolescents. In Denver, gang members committed approximately three times as many serious and violent offenses as nongang youth (Esbensen and Huizinga, 1993). Even greater differences were observed in Rochester (Bjerregaard and Smith, 1993), where gang members committed about seven times as many serious and violent delinquent acts as nongang adolescents. Seattle gang youth (ages 12–18) self-reported more than five times as many violent offenses (hitting someone, fighting, and robbery) as nongang youth (Hill et al., in press). In Rochester, two-thirds of chronic violent offenders were gang members for a time (Thornberry, Huizinga, and Loeber, 1995). As Moore (1991:132) has observed, "gangs are no longer just at the rowdy end of the continuum of local adolescent groups—they are now really outside the continuum."

How strong are the effects of gang membership on the behavior of individual members? Studies in the three cities showed that the influence of the gang on levels of youth violence is greater than the influence of other highly delinquent peers (Battin et al., 1998; Huizinga, 1997; Thornberry, 1998). Youth commit many more serious and violent acts while they are gang members than they do after they leave the gang (Esbensen and Huizinga, 1993; Hill et al., 1996; Thornberry et al., 1993). However, the influence of a gang is long lasting. In all three sites, although gang members' offense rates dropped after they left the gang, they still remained fairly high (Esbensen and Huizinga, 1993; Hill et al., 1996; Thornberry et al., 1993). Drug use and trafficking rates, the most notable exceptions to offense rate drops, remained nearly as high after members left the gang as when they were active in it (Hill et al., 1996). This study also showed that in comparison with single-year gang members, multiple-year members had much higher robbery and drug-trafficking rates while in the gang.

Gangs are highly criminogenic in certain cities and communities. Studies have not yet determined what accounts for the high levels of individual serious and violent offense rates in gangs or the lasting effects of gang involvement. Are the individual characteristics of gang members a key factor? These characteristics could be important (Yablonsky, 1962), but Esbensen, Huizinga, and Weiher (1993) found no differences in the extent to which Denver gang members, nongang street offenders, and nonoffenders were involved in eight different conventional activities: holding schoolyear jobs, holding summer jobs, attending school, and participating in school athletics, other school activities, community athletics, community activities, and religious activities. Nor have long-term studies succeeded in identifying characteristics that distinguish gang members from other serious, violent, and chronic offenders. The main difference between the two groups is gang members' higher propensity for violence (Esbensen, Huizinga, and Weiher, 1993; Horowitz, 1983; Sanchez-Jankowski, 1991; Vigil, 1988); however, this could be because more violent adolescents may be recruited into gangs.

Gang norms also constitute an important factor in the elevated level of violence in gang peer groups: "Violence that is internal to the gang, especially during group functions such as an initiation, serves to intensify the bonds among members" (Decker and Van Winkle, 1996: 270). Most gangs are governed by norms supporting the expressive use of violence to settle disputes (Short and Strodtbeck, 1965) and to achieve group goals associated with member recruitment, defense of one's identity as a gang member, turf protection and expansion, and defense of the gang's honor (Block and Block, 1993). Gang sanctioning of violence is also dictated by a code of honor that stresses the inviolability of one's manhood and defines breaches of etiquette (Horowitz, 1983; Sanchez-Jankowksi, 1991). Violence is also a means of demonstrating toughness and fighting ability and of establishing status in the gang (Short and Strodtbeck, 1965).

These norms—coupled with the fact that violence is contagious (Loftin, 1986) and clustered in space, escalates over time (Block and Block, 1991), and likely spreads more quickly among youth who are violence prone—may explain why the level of violence in gangs is higher than in other delinquent peer groups. Willingness to use violence is a key characteristic distinguishing gangs from other adolescent peer groups (Horowitz, 1983; Sanchez-Jankowski, 1991; Sanders, 1994). Violence also serves to maintain organization within the gang and to control gang members (Decker and Van Winkle, 1996; Horowitz, 1983; Sanchez-Jankowski, 1991; Yablonsky, 1962).

Levels of gang violence differ from one city to another (Miller, 1974), from one community to another (Block and Block, 1993), from one gang to another (Fagan, 1989), and even among cliques within the same gang (Moore, 1988). Violence in a particular clique changes as the group evolves: "Violence is a variable. Violence is not something inevitable and fixed with gangs" (Moore, 1988:225). Decker (1996) delineates a seven-step process that accounts for the peaks and valleys in levels of gang violence. The process begins with a loosely organized gang:

◆ Gang members feel loose bonds to the gang.

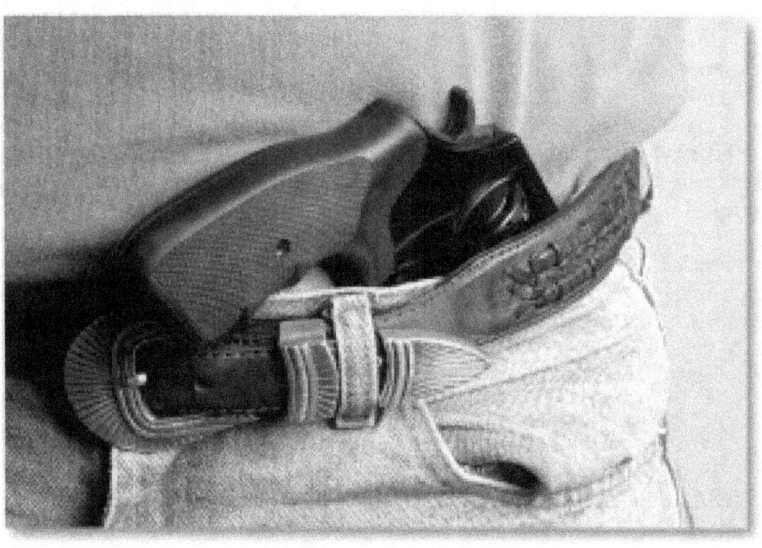

- Gang members collectively perceive a threat from a rival gang (which increases gang cohesion).

- A mobilizing event occurs—possibly, but not necessarily, violent.

- There is an escalation of activity.

- One of the gangs lashes out in violence.

- Violence and activity rapidly deescalate.

- The other gang retaliates.

Although our society has substantial basis for fearing the violence of certain gangs, most gang violence is directed at other gangs. Of nearly 1,000 gang-related homicides in Chicago from 1987 to 1994, 75 percent were intergang, 11 percent were intragang, and 14 percent involved nongang victims murdered by gang members (Block et al., 1996). Most of the intergang conflicts are concentrated in specific areas of cities with gang problems. These disputes over turf are generally played out in fights along the borders of disputed territory. Also, as Block and colleagues point out (1996:11), "Spatial analysis suggests a 'marauder' pattern, in which members of rival gangs travel to the hub of their enemy's territory in search of potential victims." Violent episodes generally occur within a mile of the attacker's residence. Rivalries with other gangs, not vengeance against society, provide the motivation for gang growth and expansion.

Guns

Adolescent propensity for violence and gun ownership and use are closely linked. Juvenile males who own guns for protection rather than for sport are six times more likely to carry guns, eight times more likely to commit a crime with a gun, four times more likely to sell drugs, almost five times more likely to be in a gang, and three times more likely to commit serious and violent crimes than youth who do not own guns for protection (Lizotte et al., 1994). Gangs are more likely to recruit adolescents who own firearms, and gang members are more than twice as likely as nongang members to own a gun for protection, more likely to have peers who own guns for protection, and more likely to carry their guns outside the home (Bjerregaard and Lizotte, 1995).

Gangs have always been armed with weapons of some sort (Newton and Zimring, 1969; Strodtbeck and Short, 1964). Recent studies have found that most violent gang members illegally own or possess a firearm (Sheley and Wright, 1993, 1995), and the lethality of assaults appears to have increased steadily (Block and Block, 1993) because of the availability and use of deadlier weapons. Gang members arm themselves because they believe their rivals have guns. According to Decker and Van Winkle (1996:23), "The proliferation of guns and shootings by gang members escalates violence by creating a demand for armaments among rival gangs." They feel they need more guns, and more sophisticated ones, so they will not be caught at a disadvantage (Horowitz, 1983).

Homicides. Although current national data on youth gang homicides is sparse, they may be following the national homicide pattern, which is in a downturn (Federal Bureau of Investigation, 1997). The growing use of more lethal weapons in gang assaults has been driving gang homicides. For example, from 1987 to 1990, virtually all of the increase in Chicago gang-motivated homicides appears to be attributable to an increase in the use of high-caliber, automatic, or semiautomatic weapons (Block and Block, 1993). The Blocks found that during a period in which there was no increase in street gang assaults, gang homicides increased, indicating that the lethality of weapons (deaths per incident) accounted for the greater number of homicides (see also Zimring, 1996). In Los Angeles, the proportion of gang-related homicides involving firearms increased from 71 percent in 1979 to 95 percent in 1994, mainly because of the increased use of handguns, particularly semiautomatics (Hutson et al., 1995). Surprisingly, assault weapons are rarely used in gang-related drive-by shootings and other homicides (Hutson, Anglin, and Pratts, 1994; Hutson et al., 1995; National Drug Intelligence Center, 1995).

National trend data on gang homicides are scant. Miller (1982) provided the first national tabulation of gang homicides, reporting a total of 633 gang-related killings in major gang cities in 1980. Since that time, gang homicides have increased dramatically, reaching epidemic proportions in certain cities like Chicago and Los Angeles.[5] The annual number of youth and adult gang-motivated homicides in Chicago increased almost fivefold between 1987 and 1994, then dropped slightly in 1995 (Block et al., 1996; Maxson, in press[a]). Youth and adult gang-related homicides in Los Angeles County more than doubled from 1987 to 1992, from 387 to 803 (Klein, 1995), dropped slightly in 1993, climbed back to the 800 level by 1995, then dropped by 20 percent in 1996 (Maxson, in press[a]). Los Angeles County Sheriff's Department data reported by the California Department of Justice (1998) also indicate this drop in gang-related homicides.

Chicago and Los Angeles alone accounted for more than 1,000 youth and adult gang homicides in 1995 (Maxson, in press[a]). Data on youth gangs in particular reveal that a member's risk of being killed is 60 times greater than that of the general population (Morales, 1992), and even higher in certain cities. For example, Decker and Van Winkle (1996) found that in St. Louis, the gang member homicide rate is 1,000 times higher than the U.S. homicide rate. National data on gang homicides were gathered in the 1995 National Youth Gang Survey (National Youth Gang Center, 1997) and again in 1996.[6]

Gang homicides have characteristics that distinguish them from nongang homicides (Maxson, Gordon, and Klein, 1985). Homicides by gang members are more likely to take place in public settings (particularly on the street), involve strangers and multiple participants, and involve automobiles (drive-by shootings). Gang homicides are three times more likely than nongang homicides to involve fear of retaliation. Unlike other homicides, gang homicides fluctuate from one racial/ethnic group to another at a given point in time and in different community areas within the same city (Block and Christakos, 1995). Gang homicide trends are also characterized by periodic spurts (Block, 1993), peaking, retreating to higher plateaus than before, then surging upward again. Spurts in gang homicides are

---

[5] Law enforcement agencies define gang homicides differently (see Maxson and Klein, 1990). In the broader definition (used in Los Angeles), "gang-related" homicide, the basic element is evidence of gang membership on the side of either the suspect or the victim. In the narrower definition (used in Chicago), a "gang-motivated" homicide is considered to be a gang crime only if the preponderance of evidence indicates that the incident grew out of a street gang function. Using the latter, more restrictive definition in counting gang homicides will produce totals about half as large as when the former, broader definition is used.

[6] OJJDP's recently published Program Summary *1995 National Youth Gang Survey*, which was prepared by the National Youth Gang Center, does not include the data collected in the survey on homicide. These data are currently being analyzed by the National Youth Gang Center, and a report is forthcoming.

explained largely by turf disputes between gangs (Block et al., 1996; Block and Block, 1993; Block and Christakos, 1995). The spurts are not citywide, but occur in specific neighborhoods and involve particular gangs. Each homicide peak tends to correspond to a series of escalating confrontations, usually over control of territory—either traditional street gang turf or an entrepreneurial drug market (Block and Christakos, 1995).[7]

Drive-by shootings. Gang-related drive-by shootings have increased in certain cities. Interestingly, killing is a secondary intent; promoting fear and intimidation among rival gangs is the primary motive (Hutson, Anglin, and Eckstein, 1996).

From 1989 through 1993, 33 percent of Los Angeles gang-related homicides were drive-bys (Hutson, Anglin, and Eckstein, 1996), resulting in 590 homicides. In Chicago, from 1965 through 1994, only 120 gang homicides resulted from drive-by shootings (about 6 percent of the total), most of which (59 percent) occurred after 1984 (Block et al., 1996).

Drug Trafficking

Although youth gangs appear to be increasing their involvement in drug trafficking, empirical research has not documented extensive networks of drug trafficking as an organized activity managed by youth gangs. The consensus among the most experienced gang researchers is that the organizational structure of the typical gang is not particularly suited to the drug-trafficking business (Klein, 1995; Moore, 1990; Spergel, 1995; Waldorf, 1993).

Some gang members become involved in drug trafficking by acting on their own, and some by involvement in gang cliques. Several researchers have identified drug-trafficking gangs and cliques within gangs established for drug distribution purposes (Decker and Van Winkle, 1996; Fagan, 1989; Sanchez-Jankowski, 1991; Skolnick et al., 1988; Taylor, 1989; Waldorf, 1993). In Chicago (Block et al., 1996), Detroit (Taylor, 1989), Milwaukee (Hagedorn, 1988, 1994a, 1994b), and San Francisco (Waldorf, 1993), a few gangs have developed lucrative drug-trafficking enterprises, and in some cases most of their violence is associated with drug trafficking. Chicago's Vice Lords and the Black Gangster Disciples are notable examples (Block and Block, 1993; Block et al., 1996).

Much has been made of the supposed relation between adolescent drug trafficking and violence (Blumstein, 1995a, 1995b; Fox, 1996). However, several gang studies have found the relation between these two behaviors to be weak or nonexistent. Despite a high prevalence of drug trafficking among Seattle gang members, accelerated adolescent involvement in drug trafficking after joining a gang, and a strong correlation between drug trafficking in midadolescence and selling drugs in late adolescence, a recent analysis of longitudinal data showed that gang involvement in drug trafficking is not a strong predictor of violence (Howell et al., in press). Several other gang studies have produced similar findings (Decker and Van Winkle, 1996; Esbensen and Huizinga; 1993; Fagan, 1989; Klein, Maxson, and Cunningham, 1991; Maxson, 1995).

Drug use, drug trafficking, and violence overlap considerably in gangs (Howell and Decker, in press). Moreover, gang involvement appears to increase individual involvement in drug use, drug trafficking, gun carrying, and violence and, perhaps, to prolong involvement in drug sales. Although drug use is strongly associated with drug trafficking, which is strongly associated with gun carrying and other serious and violent crimes, drug trafficking is not necessarily a direct cause of more frequent violent offending except in established youth and adult drug-trafficking gangs. More research is needed to resolve this issue.

Gang migration. There is some discrepancy between research results and law enforcement investigatory agency reports on youth and adult gang migration and drug trafficking (see Maxson,

Woods, and Klein, 1996). This discrepancy has many determinants, including different research methods used in the various studies, different definitions, and different information sources. Most of this gap may be accounted for by variations in definitions of gangs—and also the lack of a clear distinction between youth gangs and adult criminal organizations in reports of gang migration and drug trafficking. Some of the apparent affiliation of small local youth gangs with large gangs in major cities, indicated by similar gang names, may involve imitation or symbolism (Decker and Van Winkle, 1996). Fortunately, the gap is being narrowed, as seen through recent studies reported below.

Some possible expansion. A California study (Skolnick, 1989; Skolnick et al., 1988) suggested that the two major Los Angeles gangs, the Crips and the Bloods, were expanding their drug-trafficking operations to other cities. The National Drug Intelligence Center (NDIC) (1994) reported "a noticeable spread of Bloods/Crips gangs across the United States in the late 1980s and early 1990s." Gangs claiming affiliation with the Bloods or Crips were reported in 180 jurisdictions in 42 States. In a 1996 survey of 301 local law enforcement agencies (National Drug Intelligence Center, 1996), Chicago-based gangs were reported in 110 jurisdictions in 35 States.

Common reasons to migrate. A 1992 nationwide gang migration study of youth and adult gangs surveying 1,100 U.S. cities shows that the most common reasons to migrate (movement of members from one city to another) are social considerations, including family moves to improve the quality of life and to be near relatives and friends (Maxson, in press[b]; Maxson,

---

[7] The relation between homicide and drug trafficking will be discussed later in this Bulletin.

Woods, and Klein, 1996). Drug franchising is not the principal driving force. Migrants usually arrive individually rather than with gang companions, and existence of local gangs precedes migrating gang members in almost every instance. Only one-fifth of cities reporting gang migration attributed their gang problem to this factor. However, cities reporting gang migration said local crime rates or patterns generally were affected by migrants, primarily through increases in theft, robbery, and other violent crimes: "Gang migrants were generally not perceived as having a substantial impact on the local drug market, probably because of their relatively low numbers" (Maxson, Woods, and Klein, 1996:27). In reference to youth gangs, most gang problems are "homegrown" (Klein, 1995). Several local studies of drug-trafficking youth gangs also have not found migration to be an important factor (Decker and Van Winkle, 1996; Hagedorn, 1988; Huff, 1989; Rosenbaum and Grant, 1983; Waldorf, 1993; Zevitz and Takata, 1992; see also Maxson, in press[b]).

Drug trafficking is a small factor.
The availability of more intelligence has enabled investigatory agencies to track the movement of youth and adult gangs more precisely. The *NDIC Street Gang Symposium* (NDIC, 1995) concluded that, as the exception rather than the rule, some well-organized street gangs are engaged in interstate drug trafficking. As youth and adult gang members relocate throughout the country for various reasons, the gang's drug-trafficking connections are indirectly expanded. This new information is fairly consistent with the findings of the Maxson migration study.

It is clear that some youth gangs have extended their drug-trafficking operations to other States and cities. Their impact on local markets could be significant. Some of the migrant connections may be initiated by distant gangs for the purpose of obtaining drugs or guns (Decker and Van Winkle, 1996). However, gang migration for drug-trafficking purposes is mainly limited to within-the-region movement. Further research is needed on the impact of migrating gangs on local drug trafficking.

Homicide and the drug trade. Because the growth in youth gang violence coincided with the crack cocaine epidemic (Inciardi, 1986; Inciardi and Pottieger, 1991; Klein, 1995), the two developments appeared to be interrelated (Klein, Maxson, and Cunningham, 1991; Moore, 1990). Nonempirical assessments conducted by local governmental agencies (California Council on Criminal Justice, 1989; Skolnick et al., 1988), the U.S. Congress (Clark, 1991; General Accounting Office, 1989), and by the executive branch of the Federal Government (Bryant, 1989; Drug Enforcement Administration, 1988; Hayeslip, 1989; McKinney, 1988) concluded that gangs were instrumental in the increase in crack cocaine sales and that their involvement in drug trafficking resulted in a growth in youth violence, including homicide.

The presumed strong correlation between youth and adult gang-related homicides and drug trafficking has been questioned in several studies. Studies in Boston (Kennedy, Piehl, and Braga, 1996; Miller, 1994), Chicago (Block and Block, 1993; Block et al., 1996), Miami (Inciardi, 1990; Sampson, 1985, 1988), Los Angeles (Hutson et al., 1995; Klein, Maxson, and Cunningham, 1991; Maxson, 1995; Meehan and O'Carroll, 1992), and St. Louis (Decker and Van Winkle, 1996) consistently show a low correlation between gang-related homicides and drug trafficking (see Howell, 1997). Two caveats explain important exceptions.

First, some youth and adult gang homicides are related to the drug business, from a low of 2 percent in Chicago for the period from 1965 to 1994 (Block et al., 1996) up to 34 percent in Los Angeles for the years 1988 and 1989 (Maxson and Klein, 1996). Although most gang drug wars appear to involve adult criminal organizations, some do involve youth gangs. These can produce a large number of drug-related homicides, particularly in the case of prolonged gang wars.

Second, drug trafficking contributes indirectly to youth and adult gang homicides. Although studies indicate that drug trafficking is an infrequent cause of youth and adult gang homicide, the existence of gang drug markets provides a context in which gang homicides are more likely to occur (Hagedorn, in press). Most youth and adult gang homicides involve intergang conflicts and drug markets bring rival gang members into proximity with one another (Block et al., 1996).

There is no question that in particular communities in certain cities, youth gangs are very active in drug trafficking. However, the common stereotypes of the relationships between gangs, drug trafficking, and violence are sensationalized (Moore, 1990). Where drug-related violence occurs, it mainly stems from drug use and dealing by individual gang members and from gang member involvement in adult criminal drug distribution networks more than from drug-trafficking activities of the youth gang as an organized entity (see Howell and Decker, in press).

Youth gang homicides result more from intergang conflict than from the drug trade (Block et al., 1996; Block and Block, 1993). Most are due to impulsive and emotional defense of one's identity as a gang member, defense of the gang and gang members, defense and glorification of the reputation of the gang, gang member recruitment, and territorial disputes. Most drug distribution network groups involving youth grew out of criminal organizations formed solely for crack distribution and bear little resemblance to traditional youth gangs (Fagan, 1996; Inciardi, 1990; Moore, 1990). These findings suggest that interventions should be designed to target youth and adult gang homicides and drug trafficking as separate phenomena, except in cases in which street gang drug markets overlap with violence "hot spots" (areas with high gang crime rates) (Block et al., 1996).

Changing Composition of Youth Gangs

The popular image of youth gangs is that they are becoming more formally organized and more threatening to society, and therefore should be feared. Supergangs with thousands or tens of thousands of members, including adults, have existed at least since the 1960's (Spergel, 1995). Like other gangs, they grow in times of conflict or crisis and decrease in size at other times (Spergel, 1990). Some gangs with a high proportion of adult members have very sophisticated organizational networks, much like large corporations (see McCormick, 1996). The Black Gangster Disciples Nation (BGDN) exemplifies such an evolution from a relatively disorganized criminal street gang to a formal criminal organization (Spergel, 1995). Its corporate hierarchy (see McCormick, 1996) comprises a chairman of the board, two boards of directors (one for prisons, another for the streets), governors (who control drug trafficking within geographical areas), regents (who supply the drugs and oversee several drug-selling locations within the governors' realms), area coordinators (who collect revenues from drug-selling spots), enforcers (who beat or kill members who cheat the gang or disobey other rules), and "shorties" (youth who staff drug-selling spots and execute drug deals). From 1987 to 1994, BGDN was responsible for more than 200

Table 2: Common Differences Between Street Gangs and Drug Gangs

Street Gangs	Drug Gangs
Versatile ("cafeteria-style") crime	Crime focused on drug business
Larger structures	Smaller structures
Less cohesive	More cohesive
Looser leadership	More centralized leadership
Ill-defined roles	Market-defined roles
Code of loyalty	Requirement of loyalty
Residential territories	Sales market territories
Members may sell drugs	Members do sell drugs
Intergang rivalries	Competition controlled
Younger on average, but wider age range	Older on average, but narrower age range

Source: Klein, 1995:132.

homicides (Block et al., 1996). One-half of their arrests were for drug offenses and only one-third were for nonlethal violence.

Klein (1995:36) observed that "the old, traditional gang structure of past decades seems to be declining." In an earlier era, youth gangs might have comprised several hundred members and were generally age graded, consisting of several discrete subgroups based on age (Klein and Crawford, 1967; Moore, 1991; Miller, 1974). Both youth and adult gangs had these characteristics. Recently, however, age-graded and geographically based youth and adult gangs have become less common (see Klein and Maxson, 1996). These have given way "to relatively autonomous, smaller, independent groups, poorly organized and less territorial than used to be the case" (Klein, 1995:36). Leadership "is complex, fluid and responsive, more diffuse than concentrated, and depends in large part on the particular activity being conducted" (Miller, 1974:217). Even large youth gangs composed of allied "sets" may not be well organized and may be in a constant state of flux because of the various subgroups, changing leadership, and limited number of hardcore members (Sanders, 1994).

Although they are very much in the minority, youth and adult drug gangs are more predominant now than in the 1970's and 1980's. Klein (1995) identifies a number of common differences between youth gangs and drug gangs, recognizing that there is some overlap in these dimensions (see table 2).

The racial/ethnic composition of gangs also appears to be changing. African-American and Hispanic gangs still pre-dominate, but law enforcement agencies in a number of cities are now reporting Asian and South Pacific groups, more white gangs, and more racial/ethnic mixing than in the past (Klein, 1995).

The growth of adult prison gangs is also a fairly recent development (Ralph et al., 1996). These gangs began to be a significant factor in State prisons in the late 1960's and early 1970's, and some States are now reporting an increase in gang-related inmate violence. Moreover, there is evidence that prison gangs in Texas, for example, are exporting their operations to large urban areas in the State (Ralph et al., 1996). These developments are of concern because when adult gang member inmates return to their home communities, they give vitality to local youth gangs (Moore, 1988).

Solutions

Space limitations here preclude extensive discussion of program options.[8] Although no program has been demonstrated through rigorous evaluation (of which there has been little) to be effective in preventing or reducing serious and violent youth gang delinquency, a number of promising strategies are available.

Preventing children and adolescents from joining gangs appears be the most cost-effective long-term strategy. The Bureau of Alcohol, Tobacco and Firearms has implemented a school-based gang prevention curriculum, Gang Resistance Education and Training (G.R.E.A.T.). Evaluation has shown positive preliminary results (Esbensen and Osgood, 1997). Students who completed the G.R.E.A.T. program reported lower levels of gang affiliation and self-reported delinquency, including drug use, minor offending, property crimes, and crimes against persons. Further evaluation will determine the effectiveness of this program.

The Comprehensive Community-Wide Approach to Gang Prevention, Intervention, and Suppression Program, developed by Spergel and his colleagues (Spergel et al., 1994; see also Thornberry and Burch, 1997), contains 12 program components for the design and mobilization of community efforts by police, prosecutors, judges, probation and parole officers, corrections officers, school officials, employers, community-based agency staff such as

---

[8] See Howell (1998) for a detailed historical review of program evaluations.

street outreach workers, and a range of grassroots organization staff. Variations of this model are currently being implemented and tested in five sites under OJJDP support.

An early pilot of this model, the Gang Violence Reduction Program, has been implemented in Chicago. Preliminary evaluation results (after 3 years of program operations) are positive (Spergel and Grossman, 1997; see also Thornberry and Burch, 1997). Positive results include a lower level of serious gang violence among the targeted gangs than among comparable gangs in the area. There also is noted improvement in residents' perceptions of gang crime and police effectiveness in dealing with that crime. In addition, there are fewer arrests for serious gang crimes (especially aggravated batteries and aggravated assaults) by members of targeted gangs as compared with control youth from the same gangs and members of other gangs in Chicago. The project also was able to hasten the departure of youth from the gang while reducing their involvement in violence and other crimes (Spergel, Grossman, and Wa, 1998). These results are attributed to the project's coordinated approach combining community mobilization, suppression, and social intervention, which appears to be more effective than the traditional, mainly suppression-oriented, approach.

Studies reviewed in this Bulletin show that many serious, violent, and chronic offenders are gang members, at least at some point during adolescence. Thus, it is important for the juvenile and criminal justice systems to target gang offenders. Targeting gang members for graduated sanctions (including priority arrest, adjudication, vertical prosecution,[9] intensive probation supervision, incarceration, and transfer to the criminal justice system) can also be accomplished by implementing OJJDP's Comprehensive Strategy for Serious, Violent, and Chronic Juvenile Offenders (Howell, 1995; Wilson and Howell, 1993).

One successful intervention that can be implemented in such a comprehensive strategy is the Tri-Agency Resource Gang Enforcement Team (TARGET), which supports gang interdiction, apprehension, and prosecution. This California program integrates and coordinates the work of the Westminster Police Department, the Orange County District Attorney, and the County Probation Department (Capizzi, Cook, and Schumacher, 1995). The Gang Incident Tracking System (GITS) identifies and tracks gang members, providing the information base for the TARGET program. TARGET uses intelligence gathering and information sharing to identify and select appropriate gang members and gangs for intervention.

Police should not be expected to assume sole responsibility for gang problems, yet gang suppression remains the predominant strategy that jurisdictions use to deal with gangs. Suppression tactics have recently been expanded in three ways:

◆ State laws increasing criminal sanctions for gang crime and gang involvement and local ordinances and enforcement of specific criminal codes that restrict gang activities.

◆ Multiagency and multijurisdictional strategies bringing together several law enforcement agencies in a collective approach.

◆ Collaborative approaches tying together all sectors of the community.

A gang suppression model, the Boston Gun Project (Clark, 1997; Kennedy, Piehl, and Braga, 1996), is employing a coerced use-reduction strategy targeting gun violence involving gang members. To carry out its deterrence strategy, the Boston Police Department's Youth Violence Strike Force, through Operation Nite Lite, uses probation and police officers who patrol the streets in teams to identify gang members, enforce conditions of probation, and increase sanctions for probation and parole violations. Evaluation results are not yet available, although gun homicide victimization among 14- to 24-year-olds in the city is reported to have fallen by two-thirds after the project began (Kennedy, 1997), including a 27-month period in which no juvenile homicide occurred (Harden, 1997). Because homicides were dropping nationwide among this age group when the project began, the evaluation will compare Boston's homicide trends to a sample of other cities.

Communities should organize a collaborative approach to gang problems from the outset rather than beginning with a predominantly suppression strategy.

The program model that proves to be most effective is likely to contain multiple components, incorporating prevention, social intervention, rehabilitation, suppression, and community mobilization approaches, supported by a management information system and rigorous program evaluation.

Community responses must begin with a thorough assessment of the specific characteristics of the gangs themselves, crimes they commit, other problems they present, and the localities they affect. Other Bulletins in this series (Howell, in press) provide guidance to communities in assessing their potential gang problems and in crafting solutions. Principles for effective gang strategies are provided, along with promising and effective program models.

Conclusion

Youth gang problems are proliferating across the United States, even in small cities and towns. At the same time, the composition of youth gangs is changing. Smaller, less structured gangs are emerging, and although drug trafficking is generally not an organized activity managed by gangs, drug gangs are more predominant now than in previous decades. The racial/ethnic composition of gangs also is changing, and gangs are becoming more organized.

Gang violence—particularly homicide—has increased, owing mainly to availability and use of more dangerous weapons, especially automatic and semiautomatic handguns. This violence also has been linked to gangs' proclivity to be associated with drug trafficking. New research, however, questions the extent to which gang-related drug sales are a major cause of violence. It appears that most gang violence is related to conflicts with other gangs.

Most gang problems are homegrown. Gang migration appears to contribute little to local gang problems, including drug trafficking, except within geographic regions. There is some discrepancy between research results and investigatory agency reports on youth and adult gang migration and drug trafficking; however, much of this can be explained by the studies' use of different research methods, definitions, and information sources.

Although significant progress is being made in identifying the major risk factors for youth gang involvement, much more information is needed to specify the developmental sequence by which these risk factors operate. This knowledge will be very useful in the development of prevention and intervention programs. Progress also is being made in developing comprehensive

---

[9] The prosecutor who files a case remains responsible for it throughout the prosecution process.

programs that combine prevention, social intervention and rehabilitation, and suppression of gang violence. Because of a dearth of program evaluations, however, little is known about the effectiveness of these interventions. The current evaluation of OJJDP's five-site program may shed more light on the effectiveness of comprehensive programs.

A key issue in combating youth gangs is providing a uniform definition for them—distinguishing them from troublesome youth groups and adult criminal organizations. Youth gangs and adult criminal organizations have different origins, and they serve unique purposes for participants. Efforts to develop effective long-term interventions must take these differences into account.

References

Anderson, E. 1990. *Streetwise: Race, Class, and Change in an Urban Community.* Chicago, IL: University of Chicago Press.

Baccaglini, W.F. 1993. *Project Youth Gang-Drug Prevention: A Statewide Research Study.* Rensselaer, NY: New York State Division for Youth.

Battin, S.R., Hill, K.G., Abbott, R.D., Catalano, R.F., and Hawkins, J.D. 1998. The contribution of gang membership to delinquency beyond delinquent friends. *Criminology* 36:93–115.

Bjerregaard, B., and Lizotte, A.J. 1995. Gun ownership and gang membership. *The Journal of Criminal Law and Criminology* 86:37–58.

Bjerregaard, B., and Smith, C. 1993. Gender differences in gang participation, delinquency, and substance use. *Journal of Quantitative Criminology* 9:329–355.

Block, C.R. 1993. Lethal violence in the Chicago Latino community. In *Homicide: The Victim/Offender Connection,* edited by A.V. Wilson. Cincinnati, OH: Anderson, pp. 267–342.

Block, C.R., and Block, R. 1991. Beginning with Wolfgang: An agenda for homicide research. *Journal of Crime and Justice* 14:31–70.

Block, C.R., and Christakos, A. 1995. *Major Trends in Chicago Homicide: 1965–1994.* Research Bulletin. Chicago, IL: Illinois Criminal Justice Information Authority.

Block, C.R., Christakos, A., Jacob, A., and Przybylski, R. 1996. *Street Gangs and Crime: Patterns and Trends in Chicago.*

Research Bulletin. Chicago, IL: Illinois Criminal Justice Information Authority.

Block, R., and Block, C.R. 1993. *Street Gang Crime in Chicago.* Research in Brief. Washington, DC: U.S. Department of Justice, Office of Justice Programs, National Institute of Justice. NCJ 144782.

Blumstein, A. 1995a. Violence by young people: Why the deadly nexus? *National Institute of Justice Journal* (August):1–9.

Blumstein, A. 1995b. Youth violence, guns, and the illicit-drug industry. *Journal of Criminal Law and Criminology* 86:10–36.

Bobrowski, L.J. 1988. Collecting, organizing and reporting street gang crime. Unpublished report. Chicago, IL: Chicago Police Department, Special Functions Group.

Bryant, D. 1989 (September). *Communitywide Responses Crucial for Dealing with Youth Gangs.* Program Bulletin. Washington, DC: U.S. Department of Justice, Office of Justice Programs, Office of Juvenile Justice and Delinquency Prevention. NCJ 119465.

Bursik, R.J., Jr., and Grasmick, H.G. 1993. *Neighborhoods and Crime: The Dimension of Effective Community Control.* New York, NY: Lexington Books.

California Attorney General's Gang Unit. 1996. Number of gang members by age. Unpublished report. Los Angeles, CA: California Department of Justice, Division of Law Enforcement.

California Council on Criminal Justice. 1989. *Task Force Report on Gangs and Drugs.* Sacramento, CA: California Council on Criminal Justice.

California Department of Justice. 1998 (February). Gang-related homicides. *Intelligence Operations Bulletin* 119.

Campbell, A. 1984a. Girls' talk: The social representation of aggression by female gang members. *Criminal Justice and Behavior* 11:139–156.

Campbell, A. 1984b. Self-definition by rejection: The case of gang girls. *Social Problems* 34:451–466.

Capizzi, M., Cook, J.I., and Schumacher, M. 1995. The TARGET model: A new approach to the prosecution of gang cases. *The Prosecutor* Fall:18–21.

Chesney-Lind, M. 1993. Girls, gangs and violence: Anatomy of a backlash. *Humanity and Society* 17:321–344.

Chicago Crime Commission. 1995. Gangs: Public enemy number one, 75 years of fighting crime in Chicagoland.

Unpublished. Chicago, IL: Report of the Chicago Crime Commission.

Clark, C.S. 1991. Youth gangs. *Congressional Quarterly Research* 22:755–771.

Clark, J.R. 1997. LEN salutes its 1997 People of the Year, the Boston Gun Project Working Group. *Law Enforcement News* 23(1):4–5.

Cloward, R.A., and Ohlin, L.E. 1960. *Delinquency and Opportunity: A Theory of Delinquent Gangs.* New York, NY: The Free Press.

Cohen, A.K. 1960. *Delinquent Boys: The Culture of the Gang.* Glencoe, IL: The Free Press.

Curry, G.D. 1995a. Gang community, gang involvement, gang crime. Paper presented at the American Sociological Association Annual Meeting, Washington, DC.

Curry, G.D. 1995b (November). Responding to female gang involvement. Paper presented at the annual meeting of the American Society of Criminology, Boston, MA.

Curry, G.D. 1996. National youth gang surveys: A review of methods and findings. Unpublished. Tallahassee, FL: Report prepared for the National Youth Gang Center.

Curry, G.D., Ball, R.A., and Decker, S.H. 1996. *Estimating the National Scope of Gang Crime From Law Enforcement Data.* Research in Brief. Washington, DC: U.S. Department of Justice, Office of Justice Programs, National Institute of Justice. NCJ 161477.

Curry, G.D., Ball, R.A., Fox, R.J., and Stone, D. 1992. *National Assessment of Law Enforcement Anti-Gang Information Resources.* Final Report. Washington, DC: U.S. Department of Justice, Office of Justice Programs, National Institute of Justice. NCJ 147399.

Curry, G.D., and Decker, S.H. 1998. *Confronting Gangs: Crime and Community.* Los Angeles, CA: Roxbury.

Curry, G.D., and Spergel, I.A. 1988. Gang homicide, delinquency, and community. *Criminology* 26:381–405.

Curry, G.D., and Spergel, I.A. 1992. Gang involvement and delinquency among Hispanic and African-American adolescent males. *Journal of Research in Crime and Delinquency* 29:273–291.

Dawley, D. 1992. *A Nation of Lords: The Autobiography of the Vice Lords,* 2d ed. Prospect Heights, IL: Waveland.

Decker, S.H. 1996. Collective and normative features of gang violence. *Justice Quarterly* 13:243–264.

Decker, S.H., and Van Winkle, B. 1996. *Life in the Gang: Family, Friends, and Violence.* New York, NY: Cambridge University Press.

Drug Enforcement Administration. 1988. Crack cocaine availability and trafficking in the United States. Unpublished report. Washington, DC: U.S. Department of Justice, Drug Enforcement Administration.

Elliott, D.S. 1994. Serious violent offenders: Onset, developmental course, and termination. The American Society of Criminology 1993 Presidential Address. *Criminology* 32:1–21.

Esbensen, F., and Huizinga, D. 1993. Gangs, drugs, and delinquency in a survey of urban youth. *Criminology* 31:565–589.

Esbensen, F., Huizinga, D., and Weiher A.W. 1993. Gang and non-gang youth: Differences in explanatory variables. *Journal of Contemporary Criminal Justice* 9:94–116.

Esbensen, F., and Osgood, D.W. 1997. *National Evaluation of G.R.E.A.T.* Research in Brief. Washington, DC: U.S. Department of Justice, Office of Justice Programs, National Institute of Justice. NCJ 167264.

Fagan, J.E. 1989. The social organization of drug use and drug dealing among urban gangs. *Criminology* 27:633–669.

Fagan, J.E. 1990. Social process of delinquency and drug use among urban gangs. In *Gangs in America,* edited by C.R. Huff. Newbury Park, CA: Sage Publications, pp. 183–219.

Fagan, J.E. 1996. Gangs, drugs, and neighborhood change. In *Gangs in America,* 2d ed., edited by C.R. Huff. Thousand Oaks, CA: Sage Publications, pp. 39–74.

Federal Bureau of Investigation. 1997. *Uniform Crime Reports 1996.* Washington, DC: U.S. Department of Justice, Federal Bureau of Investigation.

Finestone, H. 1976. *Victims of Change.* Westport, CT: Greenwood.

Fox, J.A. 1996. *Trends in Juvenile Violence: A Report to the United States Attorney General on Current and Future Rates of Juvenile Offending.* Boston, MA: Northeastern University.

General Accounting Office. 1989. *Nontraditional Organized Crime.* Washington, DC: U.S. Government Printing Office.

Glasgow, D.G. 1980. *The Black Underclass: Poverty, Unemployment and Entrapment of Ghetto Youth.* San Francisco, CA: Jossey-Bass.

Gordon, R.M. 1994. Incarcerating gang members in British Columbia: A preliminary study. Unpublished study. Victoria, BC: Ministry of the Attorney General.

Hagedorn, J.M. 1988. *People and Folks: Gangs, Crime and the Underclass in a Rustbelt City.* Chicago, IL: Lakeview Press.

Hagedorn, J.M. 1994a. Homeboys, dope fiends, legits, and new jacks. *Criminology* 32:197–217.

Hagedorn, J.M. 1994b. Neighborhoods, markets, and gang drug organization. *Journal of Research in Crime and Delinquency* 31:264–294.

Hagedorn, J.M. In press. Gang violence in the post-industrial era. In *Juvenile Violence,* Crime and Justice Series, edited by M. Tonry and M. Moore. Chicago, IL: University of Chicago.

Harden, B. 1997. Boston's approach to juvenile crime encircles youth, reduces slayings. *The Washington Post* (October 23):A3.

Haskins, J. 1974. *Street Gangs: Yesterday and Today.* Wayne, PA: Hastings Books.

Hayeslip, D.W., Jr. 1989. *Local-Level Drug Enforcement: New Strategies.* Research in Action, No. 213. Washington, DC: U.S. Department of Justice, Office of Justice Programs, National Institute of Justice. NCJ 116751.

Hill, K.G., Hawkins, J.D., Catalano, R.F., Kosterman, R., Abbott, R., and Edwards, T. 1996 (November). The longitudinal dynamics of gang membership and problem behavior: A replication and extension of the Denver and Rochester gang studies in Seattle. Paper presented at the annual meeting of the American Society of Criminology, Chicago, IL.

Hill, K.G., Howell, J.C., Hawkins, J.D., and Battin, S.R. In press. Childhood risk factors for adolescent gang membership: Results from the Seattle Social Development Project. University of Washington.

Horowitz, R. 1983. *Honor and the American Dream: Culture and Identity in a Chicano Community.* New Brunswick, NJ: Rutgers University Press.

Horowitz, R., and Schwartz, G. 1974. Honor, normative ambiguity and gang violence. *American Sociological Review* 39:238–251.

Howell, J.C., ed. 1995. *Guide for Implementing the Comprehensive Strategy for Serious, Violent, and Chronic Juvenile Offenders.* Washington, DC: U.S. Department of Justice, Office of Justice Programs, Office of Juvenile Justice and Delinquency Prevention. NCJ 153571.

Howell, J.C. 1997. *Juvenile Justice and Youth Violence.* Thousand Oaks, CA: Sage Publications.

Howell, J.C. 1998. Promising programs for youth gang violence prevention and intervention. In *Serious and Violent Juvenile Offenders: Risk Factors and Successful Interventions,* edited by R. Loeber and D.P. Farrington. Thousand Oaks, CA: Sage Publications, pp. 284–312.

Howell, J.C. In press. *Youth Gang Programs and Strategies.* Bulletin. Washington, DC: U.S. Department of Justice, Office of Justice Programs, Office of Juvenile Justice and Delinquency Prevention.

Howell, J.C., and Decker, S.H. In press. *The Gangs, Drugs, and Violence Connection.* Bulletin. Washington, DC: U.S. Department of Justice, Office of Justice Programs, Office of Juvenile Justice and Delinquency Prevention.

Howell, J.C., Hill, K.G., Battin, S.R., and Hawkins, J.D. In press. *Youth Gang Involvement in Drug Trafficking and Violent Crime in Seattle.* Seattle, WA: University of Washington.

Huff, C.R. 1989. Youth gangs and public policy. *Crime and Delinquency* 35:524–537.

Huizinga, D. 1997. The volume of crime by gang and nongang members. Paper presented at the annual meeting of the American Society of Criminology, San Diego, CA.

Hutson, H.R., Anglin, D., and Eckstein, M. 1996. Drive-by shootings by violent street gangs in Los Angeles: A five-year review from 1989 to 1993. *Academic Emergency Medicine* 3:300–303.

Hutson, H.R., Anglin, D., Kyriacou, D.N., Hart, J., and Spears, K. 1995. The epidemic of gang-related homicides in Los Angeles County from 1979 through 1994. *The Journal of the American Medical Association* 274:1031–1036.

Hutson, H.R., Anglin D., and Pratts, M.J. 1994. Adolescents and children injured or killed in drive-by shootings in Los Angeles. *New England Journal of Medicine* 330:324–327.

Inciardi, J.A. 1986. *The War on Drugs: Heroin, Cocaine, Crime, and Public Policy.* Palo Alto, CA: Mayfield.

Inciardi, J.A. 1990. The crack-violence connection within a population of hardcore adolescent offenders. In *Drugs and Violence: Causes, Correlates, and Consequences,* edited by M.E. De La Rosa, Y. Lambert, and B. Gropper. NIDA Research Monograph 103. Rockville, MD: U.S. Department of Health and Human Services, National Institutes of Health, National Institute on Drug Abuse, pp. 92–111.

Inciardi, J.A., and Pottieger, A.E. 1991. Kids, crack, and crime. *Journal of Drug Issues* 21:257–270.

Johnstone, J.W. 1983. Recruitment to a youth gang. *Youth and Society* 14:281–300.

Keiser, R.L. 1969. *The Vice Lords: Warriors of the Street.* New York, NY: Holt, Rinehart and Winston.

Kennedy, D.M. 1997. Pulling levers: Chronic offenders, high-crime settings, and a theory of prevention. *Valparaiso University Law Review* 31:449–484.

Kennedy, D.M., Piehl, A.M., and Braga, A.A. 1996. Youth violence in Boston: Gun markets, serious youth offenders, and a use-reduction strategy. *Law and Contemporary Problems* 59:147–196. Special Issue.

Klein, M.W. 1995. *The American Street Gang.* New York, NY: Oxford University Press.

Klein, M.W. 1996. Gangs in the United States and Europe. *European Journal on Criminal Policy and Research* (Special Issue):63–80.

Klein, M.W., and Crawford, L.Y. 1967. Groups, gangs and cohesiveness. *Journal of Research in Crime and Delinquency* 4:63-75.

Klein, M.W., and Maxson, C.L. 1989. Street gang violence. In *Violent Crime, Violent Criminals,* edited by M.E. Wolfgang and N.A. Weiner. Newbury Park, CA: Sage Publications, pp. 198–234.

Klein, M.W., and Maxson, C.L. 1996. Gang structures, crime patterns, and police responses. Unpublished report. Los Angeles, CA: Social Science Research Institute, University of Southern California.

Klein, M.W., Maxson, C.L., and Cunningham, L.C. 1991. Crack, street gangs, and violence. *Criminology* 29:623–650.

Knox, G.W. 1991. *An Introduction to Gangs.* Barren Springs, MI: Vande Vere Publishing.

Knox, G.W., McCurrie, T.F., Laskey, J.A., and Tromanhauser, E.D. 1996. The 1996 National Law Enforcement Gang Analysis Survey: A research report from the National Gang Crime Research Center. *Journal of Gang Research* 3:41–55.

Kosterman, R., Hawkins, J.D., Hill, K.G., Abbott, R.D., Catalano, R.F., and Guo, J. 1996 (November). The developmental dynamics of gang initiation: When and why young people join gangs. Paper presented at the annual meeting of the American Society of Criminology, Chicago, IL.

Leiter, V. 1993. *Special Analysis of Data from the OJJDP Conditions of Confinement Study.* Cambridge, MA: Abt Associates.

Lizotte, A.J., Tesoriero, J.M., Thornberry, T.P., and Krohn, M.D. 1994. Patterns of adolescent firearms ownership and use. *Justice Quarterly* 11:51–73.

Loftin, C. 1986. Assaultive violence as a contagious social process. *Bulletin of the New York Academy of Medicine* 62:550–555.

Maxson, C.L. 1995 (September). *Street Gangs and Drug Sales in Two Suburban Cities.* Research in Brief. Washington, DC: U.S. Department of Justice, Office of Justice Programs, National Institute of Justice. NCJ 155185.

Maxson, C.L. In press[a]. Gang homicide. In *Homicide Studies: A Sourcebook of Social Research,* edited by D. Smith and M. Zahn. Thousand Oaks, CA: Sage Publications.

Maxson, C.L. In press[b]. *Gang Members on the Move.* Bulletin. Washington, DC: U.S. Department of Justice, Office of Justice Programs, Office of Juvenile Justice and Delinquency Prevention.

Maxson, C.L, Gordon, M.A., and Klein, M.W. 1985. Differences between gang and nongang homicides. *Criminology* 23:209–222.

Maxson, C.L., and Klein, M.W. 1990. Street gang violence: Twice as great, or half as great? In *Gangs in America,* edited by C.R. Huff. Newbury Park, CA: Sage Publications, pp. 71–100.

Maxson, C.L., and Klein, M.W. 1996. Defining gang homicide: An updated look at member and motive approaches. In *Gangs in America,* 2d ed., edited by C.R. Huff. Thousand Oaks, CA: Sage Publications, pp. 3–20.

Maxson, C.L., Woods, K., and Klein, M.W. 1996 (February). Street gang migration: How big a threat? *National Institute of Justice Journal* 230:26–31.

McCormick, J. 1996. The "Disciples" of drugs—and death. *Newsweek* (February 5):56–57.

McKinney, K.C. 1988 (September). *Juvenile Gangs: Crime and Drug Trafficking.* Bulletin. Washington, DC: U.S. Department of Justice, Office of Justice Programs, Office of Juvenile Justice and Delinquency Prevention. NCJ 113767.

Meehan, P.J., and O'Carroll, P.W. 1992. Gangs, drugs, and homicide in Los Angeles. *American Journal of the Disabled Child* 146:683–687.

Miller, W.B. 1958. Lower class culture as a generating milieu of gang delinquency. *Journal of Social Issues* 14:5–19.

Miller, W.B. 1966. Violent crimes in city gangs. *Annals of the American Academy of Political and Social Science* 364:96–112.

Miller, W.B. 1974. American youth gangs: Past and present. In *Current Perspectives on Criminal Behavior,* edited by A. Blumberg. New York, NY: Knopf, pp. 410–420.

Miller, W.B. 1975. *Violence by Youth Gangs and Youth Groups as a Crime Problem in Major American Cities.* Washington, DC: U.S. Department of Justice, Office of Justice Programs, Office of Juvenile Justice and Delinquency Prevention. NCJ 137446.

Miller, W.B. 1992. (Revised from 1982.) *Crime by Youth Gangs and Groups in the United States.* Washington, DC: U.S. Department of Justice, Office of Justice Programs, Office of Juvenile Justice and Delinquency Prevention. NCJ 156221.

Miller, W.B. 1994. Boston assaultive crime. Memorandum sent to J.C. Howell.

Miller, W.B., Geertz, H., and Cutter, H.S.G. 1962. Aggression in a boys' street-corner group. *Psychiatry* 24:283–298.

Moore, J.P. 1997. *Highlights of the 1995 National Youth Gang Survey.* Fact Sheet #63. Washington, DC: U.S. Department of Justice, Office of Justice Programs, Office of Juvenile Justice and Delinquency Prevention. FS009763.

Moore, J.P., and Terrett, C.P. In press. *Highlights of the 1996 National Youth Gang Survey.* Fact Sheet. Washington, DC: U.S. Department of Justice, Office of Justice Programs, Office of Juvenile Justice and Delinquency Prevention.

Moore, J.W. 1978. *Homeboys: Gangs, Drugs and Prison in the Barrios of Los Angeles.* Philadelphia, PA: Temple University Press.

Moore, J.W. 1985. Isolation and stigmatization in the development of an underclass: The case of Chicano gangs in East Los Angeles. *Social Problems* 33:1–13.

Moore, J.W. 1988. Introduction: Gangs and the underclass: A comparative perspective. In *People and Folks*, by J. Hagedorn. Chicago, IL: Lake View, pp. 3–17.

Moore, J.W. 1990. Gangs, drugs, and violence. In *Drugs and Violence: Causes, Correlates, and Consequences,* edited by M. De La Rosa, E.Y. Lambert, and B. Gropper. Research Monograph No. 103. Rockville, MD: National Institute on Drug Abuse, pp. 160–176.

Moore, J.W. 1991. *Going Down to the Barrio: Homeboys and Homegirls in Change.* Philadelphia, PA: Temple University Press.

Moore, J.W., and Hagedorn, J.M. 1996. What happens to girls in the gang? In *Gangs in America,* 2d ed., edited by C.R. Huff. Thousand Oaks, CA: Sage Publications, pp. 205–218.

Moore, J.W., Vigil D., and Garcia, R. 1983. Residence and territoriality in Chicano gangs. *Social Problems* 31:182–194.

Morales, A. 1992. A clinical model for the prevention of gang violence and homicide. In *Substance Abuse and Gang Violence,* edited by R.C. Cervantes. Newbury Park, CA: Sage Publications, pp. 105–118.

National Drug Intelligence Center. 1994. *Bloods and Crips Gang Survey Report.* Johnstown, PA: U.S. Department of Justice, National Drug Intelligence Center.

National Drug Intelligence Center. 1995. *NDIC Street Gang Symposium.* No. 94–M0119–002A. Johnstown, PA, November 2–3, 1994. Johnstown, PA: U.S. Department of Justice, National Drug Intelligence Center.

National Drug Intelligence Center. 1996. *National Street Gang Survey Report.* Johnstown, PA: U.S. Department of Justice, National Drug Intelligence Center.

National Youth Gang Center. 1997. *1995 National Youth Gang Survey.* Washington, DC: U.S. Department of Justice, Office of Justice Programs, Office of Juvenile Justice and Delinquency Prevention. NCJ 164728.

Needle, J., and Stapleton, W.V. 1983. *Police Handling of Youth Gangs.* Washington, DC: U.S. Department of Justice, Office of Justice Programs, Office of Juvenile Justice and Delinquency Prevention. NCJ 088927.

Newton, G.D., and Zimring, F.E. 1969. *Firearms and Violence in American Life: A Staff Report to the National Commission on the Causes and Prevention of Violence.*

Washington, DC: U.S. Government Printing Office.

Parent, D., Leiter, V., Livens L., Wentworth, D., and Stephen, K. 1994. *Conditions of Confinement: Juvenile Detention and Corrections Facilities.* Washington, DC: U.S. Department of Justice, Office of Justice Programs, Office of Juvenile Justice and Delinquency Prevention. NCJ 145793.

Pennell, S., Evans, E., Melton, R., and Hinson, S. 1994. *Down for the Set: Describing and Defining Gangs in San Diego.* San Diego, CA: Criminal Justice Research Division, Association of Governments.

Ralph, P., Hunter, R.J., Marquart, J.W., Cuvelier, S.J., and Merianos, D. 1996. Exploring the differences between gang and non-gang prisoners. In *Gangs in America,* 2d ed., edited by C.R. Huff. Thousand Oaks, CA: Sage Publications, pp. 241–256.

Redfield, R. 1941. *Folk Culture of Yucatan.* Chicago, IL: University of Chicago Press.

Rosenbaum, D.P., and Grant, J.A. 1983. *Gangs and Youth Problems in Evanston: Research Findings and Policy Options.* Evanston, IL: Center for Urban Affairs and Policy Research, Northwestern University.

Rubel, A.J. 1965. The Mexican American palomilla. *Anthropological Linguistics* 4:29–97.

Sampson, E.H. 1985 (May 14). Dade youth gangs. Final report of the Grand Jury, Circuit Court of the Eleventh Judicial Circuit of Florida in and for the County of Dade. Miami, FL: Dade County District Attorney.

Sampson, E.H. 1988 (May 11). Dade County gangs—1988. Final report of the Grand Jury, Circuit Court of the Eleventh Judicial Circuit of Florida in and for the County of Dade. Miami, FL: Dade County District Attorney.

Sanchez-Jankowski, M.S. 1991. *Islands in the Street: Gangs and American Urban Society.* Berkeley, CA: University of California Press.

Sanders, W. 1994. *Gangbangs and Drive-Bys: Grounded Culture and Juvenile Gang Violence.* New York, NY: Aldin de Gruyter.

Sante, L. 1991. *Low Life: Lures and Snares of Old New York.* New York, NY: Vintage Books.

Sheldon, H.D. 1898. The institutional activities of American children. *The American Journal of Psychology* 9:424–448.

Sheley, J.F., and Wright, J.D. 1993. *Gun Acquisition and Possession in Selected Juvenile Samples.* Research in Brief. Washington, DC: U.S. Department of Justice, Office of Justice Programs, National Institute of Justice and Office of Juvenile Justice and Delinquency Prevention. NCJ 145326.

Sheley, J.F., and Wright, J.D. 1995. *In the Line of Fire: Youth, Guns and Violence in Urban America.* Hawthorne, NY: Aldine De Gruyter.

Short, J.F., Jr. 1996. Gangs and adolescent violence. Boulder, CO: Center for the Study and Prevention of Violence.

Short, J.F., Jr., and Strodtbeck, F.L. 1965. *Group Process and Gang Delinquency.* Chicago, IL: University of Chicago.

Skolnick, J.H. 1989. Gang organization and migration—drugs, gangs, and law enforcement. Unpublished manuscript. Berkeley, CA: University of California, Berkeley.

Skolnick, J.H., Correl, T., Navarro, E., and Rabb, R. 1988. The social structure of street drug dealing. Unpublished Report to the Office of the Attorney General of the State of California. Berkeley, CA: University of California, Berkeley.

Slayton, C., Stephens, J.W., and MacKenna, D.W. 1993. *Kids Speak Out: Opinions, Attitudes, and Characteristics of Fort Worth Gang and Non-Gang Members.* Fort Worth, TX: Fort Worth Gang Research Project.

Snyder, H., and Sickmund, M. 1995. *Juvenile Offenders and Victims: A National Report.* Washington, DC: U.S. Department of Justice, Office of Justice Programs, Office of Juvenile Justice and Delinquency Prevention. NCJ 153569.

Spergel, I.A. 1990. Youth gangs: Continuity and change. In *Crime and Justice: A Review of Research,* vol. 12, edited by M. Tonry and N. Morris. Chicago, IL: University of Chicago, pp. 171–275.

Spergel, I.A. 1995. *The Youth Gang Problem.* New York, NY: Oxford University Press.

Spergel, I.A., Chance, R., Ehrensaft, K., Regulus, T., Kane, C., Laseter, R., Alexander, A., and Oh, S. 1994. *Gang Suppression and Intervention: Community Models.* Washington, DC: U.S. Department of Justice, Office of Justice Programs, Office of Juvenile Justice and Delinquency Prevention. NCJ 148202.

Spergel, I.A., and Grossman, S.F. 1997. The Little Village Project: A community approach to the gang problem. *Social Work* 42:456–470.

Spergel, I.A., Grossman, S.F., and Wa, K.M. 1998. *The Little Village Project: A Three Year Evaluation.* Chicago, IL: University of Chicago.

Strodtbeck, F.L., and Short, J.F., Jr. 1964. Aleatory risks versus short-run hedonism in explanation of gang action. *Social Problems* 12:127–140.

Sullivan, M.L. 1989. *Getting Paid: Youth Crime and Work in the Inner City.* Ithaca, NY: Cornell University Press.

Takata, S.R., and Zevitz, R.G. 1990. Divergent perceptions of group delinquency in a midwestern community: Racine's gang problem. *Youth and Society* 21:282–305.

Taylor, C.S. 1989. *Dangerous Society.* East Lansing, MI: Michigan State University Press.

Thornberry, T.P. 1998. Membership in youth gangs and involvement in serious and violent offending. In *Serious and Violent Offenders: Risk Factors and Successful Interventions,* edited by R. Loeber and D.P. Farrington. Thousand Oaks, CA: Sage Publications, pp. 147–166.

Thornberry, T.P., and Burch, J.H. 1997. *Gang Members and Delinquent Behavior.* Bulletin. Washington, DC: U.S. Department of Justice, Office of Justice Programs, Office of Juvenile Justice and Delinquency Prevention. NCJ 165154.

Thornberry, T.P., Huizinga, D., and Loeber, R. 1995. The prevention of serious delinquency and violence: Implications from the program of research on the causes and correlates of delinquency. In *A Sourcebook: Serious, Violent, and Chronic Juvenile Offenders,* edited by J.C. Howell, B. Krisberg, J.D. Hawkins, and J.J. Wilson. Thousand Oaks, CA: Sage Publications, pp. 213–237.

Thornberry, T.P., Krohn, M.D., Lizotte, A.J., and Chard-Wierschem, D. 1993. The role of juvenile gangs in facilitating delinquent behavior. *Journal of Research in Crime and Delinquency* 30:55–87.

Thrasher, F.M. 1927. *The Gang.* Chicago, IL: University of Chicago Press.

Vigil, J.D. 1988. *Barrio Gangs: Street Life and Identity in Southern California.* Austin, TX: University of Texas Press.

Vigil, J.D. 1990a. Cholos and gangs: Culture change and street youth in Los Angeles. In *Gangs in America,* edited by C.R. Huff. Newbury Park, CA: Sage Publications, pp. 116–28.

Vigil, J.D. 1990b. Street socialization, locura behavior and violence among Chicano gang members. In *Research Conference on Violence and Homicide in Hispanic Communities,* edited by J.F. Kraus, S.B. Sorenson, and P.D. Juarez. Los Angeles, CA: UCLA Publication Series.

Vigil, J.D., and Long, J.M. 1990. Emic and etic perspectives on gang culture. In *Gangs in America,* edited by C.R. Huff. Newbury Park, CA: Sage Publications, pp. 55–70.

Vigil, J.D., and Yun, S.C. 1990. Vietnamese youth gangs in Southern California. In *Gangs in America,* edited by C.R. Huff. Newbury Park, CA: Sage Publications, pp. 146–162.

Waldorf, D. 1993. Don't be your own best customer—Drug use of San Francisco gang drug sellers. *Crime, Law and Social Change* 19:1–15.

Wang, Z. 1995. Gang affiliation among Asian-American high school students: A path analysis of a social developmental model. *Journal of Gang Research* 2:1–13.

Wilson, J.J., and Howell, J.C. 1993. *Comprehensive Strategy for Serious, Violent, and Chronic Juvenile Offenders.* Washington, DC: U.S. Department of Justice, Office of Justice Programs, Office of Juvenile Justice and Delinquency Prevention. NCJ 143453.

Wilson, W.J. 1987. *The Truly Disadvantaged: The Inner City, the Underclass, and Public Policy.* Chicago, IL: University of Chicago.

Wilson, W.J. 1996. *When Work Disappears.* New York, NY: Alfred A. Knopf.

Winfree, T.L., Fuller, K., Vigil, T., and Mays, G.L. 1992. The definition and measurement of gang status: Policy implications for juvenile justice. *Juvenile and Family Court Journal* 43:29–37.

Yablonsky, L. 1962. *The Violent Gang.* New York, NY: Macmillan.

Zevitz, R.G., and Takata, S.R. 1992. Metropolitan gang influence and the emergence of group delinquency in a regional community. *Journal of Criminal Justice* 20:93–106.

Zimring, F.E. 1996. Kids, guns, and homicide: Policy notes on an age-specific epidemic. *Law and Contemporary Problems* 59:25–38. Special Issue.

James C. Howell is an Adjunct Researcher at the National Youth Gang Center, Institute for Intergovernmental Research.

This Bulletin was prepared under cooperative agreement 95–JD–MU–K001 to the Institute for Intergovernmental Research from the Office of Juvenile Justice and Delinquency Prevention, U.S. Department of Justice.

Points of view or opinions expressed in this document are those of the author and do not necessarily represent the official position or policies of OJJDP or the U.S. Department of Justice.

The Office of Juvenile Justice and Delinquency Prevention is a component of the Office of Justice Programs, which also includes the Bureau of Justice Assistance, the Bureau of Justice Statistics, the National Institute of Justice, and the Office for Victims of Crime.

Share With Your Colleagues

Unless otherwise noted, OJJDP publications are not copyright protected. We encourage you to reproduce this document, share it with your colleagues, and reprint it in your newsletter or journal. However, if you reprint, please cite OJJDP and the authors of this Bulletin. We are also interested in your feedback, such as how you received a copy, how you intend to use the information, and how OJJDP materials meet your individual or agency needs. Please direct your comments and questions to: